TOY ELEGY

For Pandelis & Julia,

"English the burning bridge"

w/ admiration,

ELIOT CARDINAUX

Eliot Cardinaux

THE BODILY PRESS
Amherst, MA

All poetry by Eliot Cardinaux except where indicated.
First Edition. Copyright © 2024 Eliot Cardinaux

This book is set in Garamond Premier Pro and Optima.
Book design and layout by Eliot Cardinaux.
eliotcardinaux.com

Cover artwork by Jeffrey Lipsky.
All Rights Reserved Copyright © 2022 Jeffrey Lipsky
"Candle Flowers."
Paints, ink, and collage on 16" x 20" canvas.
facebook.com/JLipArts

Bodily Press logo designed by Katya Popova.
popova.space

TOY ELEGY

for Jade

& for my parents

Table of Contents

From Where We Set Out / xi

BEWARE THIS HARVEST

Long Live the King / 17
In Partibus Infidelium / 18
Toy Elegy / 19
Aleph / 20
Choke / 22
Steel—Almond—Hope / 23
Admission / 24
Transit / 25
Here / 26
Memento Mori / 27
The Size of Sadness / 28
What now of the wilderness / 29
Monday / 30

THE SAME BLANK SHORE

Home Away from Home / 33
The Splitting World / 35
Kin / 39
Birds / 40
Looking Glass / 41
The Same Blank Shore / 42
Small Wordless Love / 45

◆

& THE SONG GOES ON UNSINGING EVERYTHING

Coincidence / 49
If I belong here / 50
Songtide / 51
Well-Coded Futures / 452
Sparrows / 53
& the song goes on
unsinging everything / 54

◆

SOME NEW SMALL THING

A Disentanglement / 57
Sum Value / 58
Some New Small Thing / 60
In the Alap of Dawn / 61
A Butterfly's Burden / 62
P.S. It's worth it / 63
Anima / 64
I Hear You / 65
Child / 66

◆

Acknowledgments / 69

Notes / 71

About the Author / 75

BEWARE THIS HARVEST

>   as though time had begun
>   running backward
>   into a cold and unheard of summer.
>
> —Franz Wright, *Entry in an Unknown Hand*

Long Live the King

At the end of my biography
the goats were yelling

up a wholesome pitch
the fever stirring across the board
on which the pieces had begun to move

when in droves the goats left

Here I give this witness
majesty

the whispers between sheaves
daily & daily
becoming more human

louder & louder
at the end of history

Of this the goats were dreaming

In Partibus Infidelium

inscribing how many countless years
on the underground air

the copyrighted data of our infinite
wayward music

how much dead-end light
poured in through the cracked door

we crossed paths in the ether
sighted prey

Lascaux was painted for those
whose fire kept you away

Toy Elegy

Locus, location, luster
low-sodium sister

where in zero have you been
waiting for a monostich

of color. Where in
the book have they led me

now that it's here & there
in the wind & in your hair

Such a small poor text
the shard & its magnifying

glass, in Worcester & Gloucester
the center & its mass

Where in Boston are you from?
I'm from the mentor class

The music box has not arrived
whose promises are sinister

Can you ask me what I
should & should not ask

what I know not to know
now, nothing, when it's there

Aleph

Fire, shadow walls
the frozen earth

Take this experience
& God, the scapegoat, lives

Only those strong investors
know what time will win

The ox come slowly down the hill,
the smoky carriage house

Fill the lips with volumes

In the snow stands morning
naked, drowsy, full of sleep

On a bed of straw, a nightingale
shakes out the frozen stars

A tear drawn by sunlight
gurgles like a reed-pipe
through the lashes

Oh to weep,
but only for beauty

Love will break the straw

& the grim unearthed smile
of the decade, unleashed of its nightmares,
ring

Choke

Finish the fishbone language
English
the burning bridge

Carry these customs over
on a wave of oxygen

A scapegoat concept
word freed of meaning
danger is a kind of ruin

Its long slow lilac music
resting at zero

Steel—Almond—Hope

Splayed triangle.
Bird to the eye perching aimlessly. Lash on the lam
Can I hear you saying what it means to exist in me
The book in a teapot or in the mind. The world we live in.
No right angles. Off the board this pains me
His mumbling down streets in transparent
Petropolis. Who was this third

Admission

The curtain wavers
at the dawn light

I'll only write
what needs
forgetting

The weight of a ring no longer there
on my finger

That's enough

Still wary of the plughole
I hear myself clamoring for light
between you & yourself in the wall

Transit

into the unfortunate
light of day

the sun-damaged
march of morning

is it red
to beware this harvest

below the map
where the notes of heaven

intricate
drowsy & latent now are gone

what does this skeleton
reach for in the dust around it

every cell marches forward
braces toward winter shining

our bright stasis
emptied of all of it

Here

Where you can't
imagine me

October turns the hillside
pale
  & backwards green

At night
in the sleepless order
  of the house,
beneath the dogeared sheets
the city mourns you.

Glares above my dream.

If a crisis had eyes,
her lights
would open them

Don't wait for fate
to place your memory
back on the street

Some days I lean
like a fisherman
& float out in

Memento Mori

His name came out in white

A void in graphite
left by depression in lichened
slate

The wild leaves

A field on fire
lighting up the walnut-inside
of my head

Then the world returned

A fear uncertain
where it came from

Candy-bright green
gas station plastic, cloying
to catch the attention of no one

The Size of Sadness

So many similarities
between us
the crow & the kestrel

One provides for another
& yet has to fight to rest
in an upper branch

Between a poplar
that is no longer there
& one whose leaves are still there
shimmering & quaking

When one leaf falls
this is how we tell the difference

When one leaf falls

How different from a life this is

What now of the wilderness

dream become phantom
limb

awoken in ashen comfort
by grey rain

reached for the stillness
of sloping pine

raised high above
your hearing

vertigo of a scream
the enduring fantasy

Monday

The itchy fibers of my coat
returned to their display

To relish this world,
its stored-up sea

this district insinuated,
woven from real & translated
cities

the greylong glare of it
staring out the horror
from my eyes

This is how I know you
to live forever

noise from the kettle

the silence of scraps of paper
holding vigil for the waves

THE SAME BLANK SHORE

From above: invisible and uncertain.
From below: from the abyss of hope
for the distant, the future-distant kin.

—Paul Celan, *Microliths*

Home Away from Home

Another thirteenth passes
without a Friday

with the quiet of cornflower,
death-quiet blue

In the linger-tone of our yellow house

dust's memory sniffs toward the crying green
outward from inside air

lost in time as time is allowed to be

Music from passing cars
programs the light haze of not-quite-summer
not-quite fall

to code the endearing berries
onto the fixed disawning

paint of our days
a forbidden ambling

white like the beard of a shopkeep
baking bread

It twists inside the noun
three vowels of ecstasy

There appears
a question

in which I re-enter
my own calligraphy

The Splitting World

I.
Long have we been here

Our sameness hurts the rose of winter

The ruts grow deep enough to sow
the ruined road

Beneath the undercutting
gaze of sleep
the bone unfurls

Sheds its letters speechless
along the mesh

II.
We wake to hear
in music

We are not
simply of this earth

That the daylight yearns
the shards of night we cement
together

Into the seed to sow

III.
They are not my tears
that sing like this involuntarily

Learning the poem enclosed by day
half-bound to sleep

To bathe our eyes
in its splitting world

IV.
What tree is this

Our sky tastes its rhythmic leaves

You move in the chapped
silence

A balm of noise

Kin

after Paul Celan

I.
THRESHOLD TO THRESHOLD

you grapple & cross it.
Bars on the night sky.
A skeleton whose words you use
to fill the night with hydrogen
collapses. Bars on the night sky

II.
INFINITE LIKE THE COSMOS

it stands adjacent
without who made it.

The hope of it found me

Birds

Their footprints
scattered language
in the snow

Algiz
Eolhx

Yew or Elk

Elhaz

The life-rune

ᛉ

ts

ks

Inverted,
the death-rune

ᛦ

yr

Storm-detachment.
Brownshirts

Looking Glass

Rumors, like snowfall.
No heaven, no earth.
Let me move more
swiftly inside
life's double intricacy.
Down to the corner
to lean on a rail.
Let night come. To live on the street.
A raspberry snow globe.
The sighs & yawns
of a mother
puttering on her own in the
house. No sign of it ceasing,
all this snow. The purple
exhaustion of brown stone
lit up by a street lamp.
The night is day.
I can't see so far as to live.

The Same Blank Shore

for Katya Popova

I.
The sound of a low-flying jet
didn't mesh with the traffic

A green light blinking
never seen that but
it's calm here

Looks like a prison
probably a barracks

I long to intermesh these
towns, these
narrow oxygens

Carry the present past

II.
A paper balloon
like the sound of sleep

Back home but where is it

A tear along the horizon
reveals the horizon

Am I the same
blank shore

III.
Overnight I feel it.
I feel into paper,
fighting with birds & their shape

To come to the other
side & make some strange
sense sound like a heartbeat

Swishing with snow-covered
spruce boughs the world is
overwhite

Small Wordless Love

for Sarah Menefee

I think I'll stare at this. A small
wordless love. I think I'll stare at this
music. Maybe that'll pass.
A small wordless love
that seeks to pass.
Pass over what it hovers
over, pass away eventually.
Everything passes away.
I think I'll hold this
in my attention. This
small wordless love.
Make ready for your gifts.
Make ready. Everything
passes away.

& THE SONG GOES ON UNSINGING EVERYTHING

> What is good? Is it the sun?
> The old wood drying in the sun?
> Is it this immense, vaulting
> blue-blinding blue winter sky?
>
> —Patrick Pritchett, *Refrain Series*

Coincidence

I have held the shattered alphabet
corrected in what I hope
were your crying eyes. She
sang to me as if she wanted for me
to be still the same. Now
it has begun to rain. The sound of it
is easy to understand as
she cuts my hair.

If I belong here

in your troubled heaven
beside
the lavender

not for the war
raging out of your mother's
memory

not for her brother
returning

I was not him

& the horses
you sang of

pintos
dapples & greys

I will not think
the only good in this

Songtide

The inhuman
humor of goat screams.
Nights like these I am a shore
for music to wash up on. Song that pulls
away from the droning of tree frogs.
This one a march of angels.
This one a clenched jaw dredging
up a clamor of church bells. Dishes
clatter. There's not enough chaos
in this house to start a fire. Long
live the king. Words that
rumble at the sight of rain.

Well-Coded Futures

after René Char

To outlive
the enclosure of tragedy

The dilapidated fences,
quarantine long over,
burn

Cloud of resistance
dragging hypnosis behind you

Nothing is holding you here

SOME NEW SMALL THING

If exit is merely a sign

—Peter Gizzi, *The Outernationale*

A Disentanglement

I.
TOGETHER

the rocks make a sign. The
sun in a field of grass. I wintered
over in this place of purpose.

II.
OFF THE LEDGE OF MEANING

This trough was reserved for you.

III.
BIRDSONG

bed down light's
architecture of pain

in
commotion's cradle

a word
one sliver of sound has
totaled
the darkness

Sum Value

for Peter Gizzi

You opened among the roses

Sunlight, silver of the haunting
runoff from a two-way trip

Who will follow in
this idea of light. Agape
reflection of the moon

why shadow
sleeps on becoming light
the proof of its brightness

where a spray of pine wakes
in a mineshaft

the paleontologist's
eye, etched on a curve
of jawbone, the matte of plaster

instrumental music, drumming
what is good enough

In the frantic
summit of the afternoon

a newspaper at the center
flown
from its windblown pages

I rest in the amber vista
of your voice

as if to begin
tearing wanness
out of the light

tonight I dreamt the beloved
into being

Some New Small Thing

School is letting out. Soon
this town will be asleep
in the drowsy summer
air. Sometimes I wonder
if it's sad to be adjusted
to this world. Tonight I heard
a far-off whistle or a child,
maybe a coyote cry, while
we carried Lenten roses
out to the car. As a friend
blurted out, I'm doing it.
Just to get the blood going. If
that's what it means to keep things
simple. When a kiss is a far-off thing.

In the Alap of Dawn

You remember the alap of dawn
walking through the town. A rumor of
unheard music, unseen things. &
told of it somehow you were better off
for not hearing what was said.

A Butterfly's Burden

for Tom Snarsky

Do you know your beauty
come to visit me?

In a sharpness
of samara dust

I let her mow a circle
around one tree

P.S. It's worth it

As long as there is hearing in the body.
This is not an anechoic

Cage. Blood bass, nerve treble. Not
a temple but a shrine in a landscape

Hummingbird heart in the universe.
As long as there is feeling in the body.

As long as there's a body. Space
for a body, body of water, politic

Reserve the right to blaspheme.
This life on earth is why everything hurts

Anima

When silence stood, like a tall
man in a cool, dark hallway

There you were, making small
sounds. A ping for feeling

The window open, smoke
filling the air whispered

Continuity. There is not
much I can say. I'm sorry

For how the song turned
out. Come crawling from

Under a chair to hear it
the day we meet.

I Hear You

*for Jeb Bishop
& Flin van Hemmen*

The whole world rings
in your ears every time

you stop. & listen to
the sound of the birds.

They are chipper, even
chirping the same note

over & over. Avoiding
repetition somehow.

The sun's note is different.
A blue-bellied warship

floats under circling
hawks & makes a buzz

like an insect in the heart
of the day. Keep building

the world out of tinker-
toy language. Even as it burns.

Site

for Caleb Schmale

Child
in relation to no one

●

Creak
of a swing
warm vertigo

●

Familiar
perspective
loss of balance

●

You forget
cities almost
move on too

●

Evidence
in these shards
of laughter

●

Each
forms
the extending present

Acknowledgments

My sincere thanks to the editors of the following journals in which these poems first appeared:

"Long Live the King," "In Partibus Infidelium," and "Admission" in *Fortnightly Review*.

"Toy Elegy" in *Spectra Online*.

"Here" in *Rejected Lit*.

"Home Away from Home," "The Splitting World," and "A Disentanglement" in *Meat for Tea*.

"Kin" and "Looking Glass" in *Meridian*.

"Coincidence," "Songtide," and "Sparrows" in *Trestle Ties*.

"Site" in *California Quarterly*, as "Child," alongside "& the song goes on unsinging everything."

Poems in this collection also appeared in the following chapbooks from The Bodily Press: *Apparitions* (2023); *Split World* (2023); *The Life in Pictures* (2023); and *Take 1* (2023).

The poems "Toy Elegy," "The Splitting World," "Kin," "Birds," "The Same Blank Shore," and "Small Wordless Love" also appear on the album *Imminence* (self-released, 2024) with Gary Fieldman on percussion, and the author on piano. The album was co-produced by the musicians, with Warren Amerman. My thanks to Gary and Warren for inviting the poetry in.

My gratitude to Sean Ali, whose drawings graced the pages of the chapbook *Apparitions* (Bodily Press, 2023), alongside the poems in the first section of this book.

My deepest gratitude to Ivy Schweitzer for her friendship, and for being a first reader of this collection.

Special thanks to Jeffrey Lipsky for the generous use of his original artwork, inspired by several of my previous chapbooks on which his artworks also appeared.

Deep bow to Peter Gizzi, whose elegy is fierce, to Sarah Menefee, whose love is big and full of words, and to Patrick Pritchett, whose logos is always flickering.

My deep respect and gratitude to Pierre Joris for the 52 years' labor he devoted to Paul Celan scholarship and translation, without whose fruits my own project in great part would not exist.

Love and thanks to Tom Snarsky, Jo Ianni, and Adrian Lürssen for their friendship, for believing in my work, and for texting poetics long into the night.

Thank you to Jeb Bishop and Flin van Hemmen for hearing me, to Caleb Schmale for holding space in Boston, and to Katya Popova for putting me up in her North Shore hovel.

Finally, a heartfelt thank you to my ever-present family.

Notes

The epigraphs at the beginning of this collection are taken respectively from René Char's poem "Every Life..." ("*Toute Vie...*"), as translated by James Wright and collected in *Selected Poems of René Char*, edited by Mary Ann Caws and Tina Jolas (New Directions, 1992); and from Bei Dao's poem "Year's End," as translated by David Hinton and collected in *At the Sky's Edge* (New Directions, 2001).

The epigraphs at the beginning of each section of this collection are taken respectively from the following books: Franz Wright's *Entry in an Unknown Hand* (Carnegie Mellon University Press, 1989); Paul Celan's *Microliths They Are, Little Stones: Posthumous Prose*, Pierre Joris, translator (Contra Mundum, 2020); Patrick Pritchett's *Refrain Series* (Dos Madres, 2020); and Peter Gizzi's *The Outernationale* (Wesleyan University Press, 2008).

In the foreword, "From Where We Set Out," the Latin, "*Assum est. Versa et manduca*," translates roughly, "It's done. Turn it over and take a bite." The quote is attributed to Saint Lawrence, a 3rd Century Christian martyr roasted over an open flame for having distributed the church's money to the people, rather than having it stolen by a Roman state actor. "Lucile" is a character in Georg Büchner's play, *Danton's Death*, collected in *Danton's Death, Leonce and Lena, Woyzeck* (Oxford University Press, 1998). The title "Long Live the King" is a line in *Danton's Death*, spoken by Lucile. Paul Celan, in his *Meridian* address, given on receipt of the Georg Büchner Prize in 1960, calls this line "poetry." In it, he says, "homage is being paid to the majesty of the absurd as witness for the presence of the human." Source: *The Meridian: Final Version—Drafts—Materials*, Pierre Joris, translator; Bernhard Böschenstein/Heino Schmull, editors (Stanford University Press, 2011).

The title "In Partibus Infidelium" is borrowed from a fragment in Paul Celan's *Microliths* (Contra Mundum), which reads, "the poet: always in partibus infidelium." The Latin translates, "in the land of the non-believers."

The title "Steel—Almond—Hope" derives from the names of the Soviet dictator Joseph Stalin (the Russian *"Stal"* for "steel"), the Russian poet Osip Mandelstam (the German *"Mandel"* for "almond"), and the first names of both of their wives (the Russian "Nadezhda," meaning "hope"). Stalin imprisoned and exiled Mandelstam for having written an epigram denouncing him. Mandelstam died of typhoid fever in a transit camp near Vladivostok, in 1938. Nadezhda Alliluyeva, Stalin's second wife, committed suicide in 1932, while Mandelstam's wife, Nadezhda Yakovlevna Mandelstam (*née* Khazina), wrote several harrowing memoirs of their life together, and also memorized, hid, and helped smuggle all of her deceased husband's poems to America, where they were eventually published in full, and later translated into English. The phrase "transparent Petropolis" (referring to Mandelstam's beloved city of Saint Petersburg), is from the poet's second collection, *Tristia*, Kevin Kinsella, translator (Green Integer, 2007).

The poem "Toy Elegy" makes use of ideas discussed in Patrick Pritchett's essay, "How to Write Poetry After Auschwitz: The Burnt Book of Michael Palmer," collected in *Make it Broken: Toward a Poetics of Late Modernism* (Black Square Editions, 2025). The poem derives loosely from Michael Palmer's *Little Elegies for Sister Satan* (New Directions, 2021).

The title "The Size of Sadness" is a phrase from Bei Dao's poem "To My Father," collected in *The Rose of Time: New and Selected Poems*, Eliot Weinberger, editor and translator; Yanbing Chen, translator (New Directions, 2009).

The subtitles of "Kin" are borrowed from Paul Celan. *Threshold to Threshold* is the title of one of his books, collected in *Memory Rose into Threshold Speech: The Collected Earlier Poetry*, Pierre Joris, translator (FSG, 2020). "Infinite like the cosmos" describes the "old, eternal [distances ...] like the distance between one's I and one's You," from a fragment collected in *Microliths* (Contra Mundum).

In the poem "Birds," "ᛉ"(Elhaz or Algiz, meaning "Elk" or "Yew") is the 15th letter in the Futhark runic alphabet. Appropriated by the Nazis, and by subsequent far-right movements, the symbol was used by the Third Reich to signify life, often on birth records, though its applications were manifold. Inverted ("ᛉ"), the rune was similarly used to signify death. Both are still considered hate symbols when used by the far-right, though they are also used in Pagan cultures. Source: Anti-Defamation League (https://www.adl.org), and the Wikipedia entry for "Algiz."

The poem "Sum Value" makes its title from Peter Gizzi's collection, *Some Values of Landscape and Weather* (Wesleyan University Press, 2003).

The title of the poem "A Butterfly's Burden" is borrowed from that of a book by the Palestinian poet Mahmoud Darwish, *The Butterfly's Burden*, Fady Joudah, translator (Copper Canyon, 2007).

In the poem "P.S. It's worth it," the phrase "anechoic / Cage" refers to American composer John Cage's experience of entering a 'soundless' anechoic chamber, in which, despite the silence, he still heard the low pulse of his own blood, and the high-pitched thrum of his own nervous system. Source: *Indeterminacy: New Aspect of Form in Instrumental and Electronic Music. Ninety Stories by John Cage, with Music*, with pianist David Tudor (Smithsonian/Folkways, 1959).

In the same poem, the line "not a temple but a shrine in a landscape" derives from a fragment in Paul Celan's *Microliths* (Contra Mundum), which reads, "Endnote: Poetry 'a shrine with no temple.'" The line "reserve the right to blaspheme" is taken from a letter written by Paul Celan to Nelly Sachs, collected in *Paul Celan, Nelly Sachs: Correspondence*, Barbara Wiedemann, editor (Syracuse University Press, 1995). When Sachs asked Celan whether he was a believer, he simply replied, "I reserve the right to blaspheme."

About the Author

ELIOT CARDINAUX is a poet, pianist, composer, and translator working at the edges of the lyric and improvised music. The author of *On the Long Blue Night* (Dos Madres, 2023), and the trio of *Quiet Labor*, *Toy Elegy*, and *This Music From Another Room* (Bodily Press, 2024), as well as numerous chapbooks, Cardinaux has also produced and appeared on over a dozen albums of original music, including *American Thicket* (Loyal Label, 2016); *Out of Our Systems* and *Pavane* (Bodily Press, 2022); and most recently *Imminence* (self-released, 2024) with American percussionist Gary Fieldman. He holds a bachelor's degree in contemporary improvisation from The New England Conservatory of Music, and an MFA in creative writing, with a focus on poetry, from the University of Massachusetts in Amherst. Eliot's poems and translations have appeared in journals such as *California Quarterly*, *Tupelo Quarterly*, *Meridian*, *Jacket2*, *The Arts Fuse*, *Bennington Review*, *Solstice*, and *Spoon River Poetry Review*. At present, he co-leads an American trio with bassist Will McEvoy and drummer Max Goldman, works in a duo with Gary Fieldman, leads his own Danish Quartet, and is a member of the European-based free-improvisation ensemble, Our Hearts as Thieves. He has appeared, in various settings, with musicians such as Kresten Osgood, Mat Maneri, Randy Peterson, Thomas Morgan, Asger Thomsen, Ryan Blotnick, Eivind Opsvik, Niels Vincentz, Taus Bregnhøj-Olesen, Isaac Luxon, Flin van Hemmen, and Mia Dyberg. He performs throughout Europe and the Northeast United States. He has taught literature and writing at UMass Amherst, and works as a bookseller at Amherst Books. He is the sole founder and editor of The Bodily Press.

Author photograph by poet Denver Butson • denverbutson.com

THE BODILY PRESS
bodilypress.bandcamp.com